CONTENTS OF THE BOOK:

ABOUT THE AUTHOR:

VIVEK KR AGRAWAL, is a member of The Institute of Chartered Accountants of India. He is fellow member of the Institute. He has the experience of more than 10 years in the field of Tax Consultancy. He secured All India Rank in his CA exams. He has also qualified L.L.B., Diploma in Insurance & Risk Management and Diploma in Information System Audit. Associated in different capacities with several Professional Institutes, Management colleges and Business houses in India and abroad. He can be reached at *vivek.vka@gmail.com*.

INTRODUCTION

The Goods and Services Tax (GST) the biggest reform in Indirect taxation of India has been rolled out from 01st July, 2017. It extends to whole of India. It is based on the principle of **destination-based consumption** taxation.

By the Constitution amendments passed in parliament and ratified by various state, now the Central and State governments will have simultaneous powers to levy the GST on Intra-State supply. Though the Parliament alone shall have exclusive power to make laws with respect to levy of Goods and Services Tax on Inter-State supply. GST to be levied by the Centre on intra-state supply would be called Central GST (CGST) and that to be levied by the States would be called State GST (SGST). An Integrated GST (IGST) would be levied an inter-state supply of goods or services.

As the government wants to have unified tax structure across the country the cooperation is required from every state on various matter, so The Goods and Service Tax Council **(GSTC)** was formed. GSTC comprises of the Union Finance Minister, the Minister of State (Revenue) and the State Finance Ministers to recommend on the GST rate, exemption and thresholds, taxes to be subsumed and other matters.

The whole GST system will be backed by a robust IT system. In this regard, Goods and Services Tax Network **(GSTN)** has been set up by the Government. It will provide front end services and will also develop back end IT modules for States who opted for the same.

Major taxes subsumed in GST are:

- Central Excise Duty
- Duties of Excise (Medicinal and Toilet Preparations)
- Additional Duties of Customs (CVD)
- Special Additional Duty of Customs (SAD)
- Service Tax
- State Value Added Tax (VAT)
- Central Sales Tax (CST)
- Entry Tax
- Purchase Tax
- Luxury Tax
- Taxes on lotteries, betting and gambling

GST would apply on all goods and services except Alcohol for human consumption. GST on five specified petroleum products (Crude, Petrol, Diesel, ATF & Natural Gas) would by applicable from a date to be recommended by the GST Council.

Below a simple example to explain the significance of various terms and topics to be covered going forward.

Example – On 10th August 2017 Rahul from Mumbai has purchased laptop from Flipkart, Bengaluru for Rs 40,000. The market price of product is Rs 50,000/-. The tax rate is 18%.

Question: Is this transaction liable to GST?
Answer: To know this we need to understand the basic structure of gst, meaning of supply and related concepts.

Question: Who needs to pay GST?
Answer: Basic concept and Reverse charge mechanism.

Question: On what value of amount, tax rate will apply?
Answer: Value of Supply topic.

Question: Whether CGST-SGST or IGST needs to be charged?
Answer: Place of Supply topic.

Question: When is liability to pay tax to the tax department arise?
Answer: Time of Supply topic.

Question: How to pay the tax?
Answer: Input Tax Credit and Payment of tax topic.

Question: What proof should be kept of the transaction for future purpose?
Answer: Invoicing, Accounts and Records topic.

Question: What related compliances needs to be done?
Answer: GST returns topic.

Another simple example to elucidate the working, calculation and disclosure of GST on within state sale (intra-state sale) and out of state sale (inter-state sale).

Example: Rajesh sold the goods to Mahesh for Rs 10,000. GST rate is 18%. Both are located in Karnataka.

Answer:

Value of goods – Rs 10,000
CGST @ 9% – Rs 900
SGST @ 9% – Rs 900
Gross Value – Rs 11,800

18% will be bifurcated into CGST and SGST equally

.

Example: Ranbir, Mumbai sold the goods to Rajni, Chennai for Rs 10,000. GST rate is 18%.

Answer:

Value of goods – Rs 10,000
IGST @ 18% – Rs 1800
Gross Value – Rs 11,800

CONCEPT OF "SUPPLY"

A **taxable event** is any event or occurrence that results in a tax liability. The taxable event in GST is supply of goods or services or both. So the first and the foremost condition to make transaction taxable to GST is **Supply**.

Various taxable events like manufacture(for excise), sale(for VAT), rendering of service(for Service tax), purchase(for purchase tax), entry into a territory of state(for Entry tax) and many other have been done away with in favour of just one event i.e. Supply.

In general words, Supply means To Provide. It includes sale, transfer, barter, exchange, license, rental, lease or disposal.

TRANSACTION LIABLE TO GST

Now we discuss few general universal condition to be fulfilled by a transaction to make it chargeable/taxable to GST. This can be better understood in terms of following six parameters:

1. Supply of **goods or services**. Supply of anything other than goods or services does not attract GST. So it is important to know what is Goods and what is Services (Covered under Definition Chapter)

2. Supply should be made for a **consideration** (a payment or reward). It is immaterial whether the payment is made by the recipient or by any other person.

Example – Tata Motors sold a car to Abhishek Bachchan, the car was registered under his name. The payment for the car was however made by Amitabh Bachchan. Is the selling of the car to Abhishek Bachchan considered as Supply? Answer is YES.

3. Supply should be made in the **course or furtherance of business**. That is personal dealing won't be regarded as supply.

Example - A Dealer of Cement buys cement for trading, is considered as Supply.

Example – The same dealer if buys laptop to keep accounting of the stock, this buying of laptop of his business will also be regarded as Supply, as it will be used in the furtherance of his business.

Example – A homemaker lady selling of old newspaper or plastic waste to raddiwala won't be considered as supply. As the lady is just selling the unusable material on her house which is primarily not for business purpose.

Example – A lady went to Jewellery shop to sell her old jewels. As she is not a regular dealer selling jewellery, this won't be considered as supply under GST.

4. Supply should be made by a **taxable person**.

A "taxable person" is a person who is **registered** or **liable to be registered** under the GST law. Hence, even an unregistered person who is liable to be registered is a taxable person. Similarly, a person not liable to be registered but has taken voluntary registration and got himself registered is also a taxable person.

Example – A dealer having a turnover of Rs 2 lakh pa only and has taken GST registration shall be considered as a taxable person, even if his turnover is below threshold limit.

5. Supply should be a **taxable supply**. GST will not be charged on non-taxable supply or exempt supply.

Example – Prasadam supplied by religious places is an exempt supply. Hence, no gst will be charged on selling or giving of prasadam to devotee.

6. Supply should be made within the **taxable territory**. So the place of supply should be in India.

Example – Bill gates selling his software to Warren Buffett in US won't be considered as taxable under Indian GST.

To charge GST – Transaction should be a supply of the taxable goods or services or both by a taxable person in the taxable territory for consideration in the course or furtherance of business.

<u>IS THIS GOODS OR SERVICES??</u>

Sometimes there might be a confusion as to whether the transaction is a supply of goods or supply of service. Example- Photography. The photographer provides the photo (goods) but at the same time it can be said that he is providing services of clicking and converting to photo with the paper cost being very low as compared to the price charged.

It is essential to bifurcate as this classification might decide the exemption or tax rate.

The GST law to minimize this uncertainty lists a few specific activities which are specifically be treated as supply of goods or supply of services which are detailed below:

1. Transfer of the **title** in goods (ownership) or under an agreement which stipulates that property in goods shall pass at a future date upon payment of full consideration as agreed, is a supply of goods.

Example – Raj makes an agreement with Anjali to sell his car after 3 month on payment of Rs 5 lakhs. This has shall be considered as supply of goods and not supply of services even if title has not been passed to Anjali today.

2. Transfer of **right** in goods without the transfer of title is a supply of services.

Example – Company hiring a laptop on rental basis. The company has authority to use the laptop as per their will but the ownership is still with the shopkeeper. This will be regarded as supply of services and not goods, even though the laptop is goods.

3. Supply of goods by any unincorporated association or body of persons to a member shall be treated as supply of goods.

Example – A partnership firm giving some of its asset or goods to partner shall be considered as supply.

4. Any lease, tenancy, easement, license to occupy land is a supply of services.

5. Any lease or letting out of the building including a commercial, industrial or residential complex for **business or commerce**, either wholly or partly, is a supply of services.

6. Transfer of Business Assets under the directions of the person carrying on the business so as no longer to form part of those assets, whether or not for a consideration, is a supply of goods.

7. Below list shall also be treated as Services:

- Renting of immovable property.

- Any treatment or process which is applied to another person's goods, construction of a complex, building, civil structure or a part thereof, including a complex or building intended for sale to a buyer, wholly or partly.

- **Temporary** transfer or permitting the use or enjoyment of any intellectual property right.

- Development, design, programming, customisation, adaptation, upgradation, enhancement, implementation of information technology software.

- Agreeing to the obligation to refrain from an act, or to tolerate an act or a situation, or to do an act.

- Transfer of the **right** to use any **goods** for any purpose (whether or not for a specified period).

- Composite Supply – **Works Contract** and Supply of goods: being **food** or any other article for human consumption or any **drink**.

Examples:

- ➢ Taking an office space on rent is Services.
- ➢ Repairing a vehicle belonging to other is Services.
- ➢ Permitting the use of patent to manufacture the product is Services.
- ➢ Development of customized software is Services.
- ➢ Giving the bike on rent for one day is Services.
- ➢ Works Contract, a mixture of service and transfer of goods is regarded as Services.
- ➢ Hiring contractor for building premises is Services.
- ➢ Restaurants providing food is considered Services.

<u>**NEITHER A SUPPY OF GOODS NOR SERVICES**</u>

Further on few activities or transactions government do not intend to charge the tax and hence they have listed activities or transactions which shall not be treated as a supply of goods or services i.e. non-taxable supply:

1. Services by an employee to the employer in the **course of or in relation** to his employment. No GST has to be paid/collected while paying salary.

2. Services by any court or Tribunal established under any law. As they help parties resolving the disputed matter. To keep the justice at low cost this has been kept out of GST.

3. The functions performed by the Members of Parliament, Members of State Legislature, Members of Panchayats, Members of Municipalities and Members of other local authorities.

4. Services of funeral, burial, crematorium or mortuary including transportation of the deceased. The government is merciful and desire that death should be tax free and hence no GST once the person leaves the taxable territory.

5. Sale of land and Sale of building where the entire consideration has been received after completion certificate is issued or after its first occupation. The relevant stamp duty and state taxes needs to be paid. More on this will be discussed in upcoming chapters.

6. Actionable claims, other than lottery, betting and gambling. Actionable claim is a claim to any debt (except secured debts) which the civil courts recognize as affording grounds of relief.

COMPOSITE AND MIXED SUPPLIES

A composite supply means a supply comprising two or more supplies of goods or services or any combination thereof, which are **naturally bundled** and supplied in conjunction with each other in the **ordinary course of business**, *one* of which is a **principal supply**.

Example — A travel ticket from Mumbai to Delhi may include service of food being served on board, free insurance, and the use of airport lounge. In this case, the **transport of passenger**, constitutes the pre-dominant element of the composite supply, and is treated as the **principal supply** and all other supplies are ancillary.

Mixed supply means two or more **individual** supplies of goods or services, or any combination, made in conjunction with each other for a **single price**.

Example — A package consisting of canned foods, sweets, chocolates, cakes, dry fruits, aerated drinks and fruit juices when supplied for a single price is a mixed supply; as each of these items can be supplied separately and is not dependent on any other.

The GST Law lays down the tax liability on a composite or mixed supply in the following manner.

1. **Composite Supply** comprising two or more supplies one of which, is a principal supply, shall be treated as **supply of such principal supply**. In case of above example tax rate applicable on Transport of passenger will be applicable to the price charged.

2. **Mixed Supply** comprising two or more supplies, shall be treated as supply of that particular supply which attracts the **highest rate of tax**.

Example — A package worth Rs 2000 containing - Cashew nuts (5%), Almond (12%) and Chocolate Biscuits packet (18%).

As chocolate biscuits attracts the highest rate of rate eighteen percent among other goods in the package, Tax will be charged 18% on Rs 2000/-.

Bird's eye view of topic covered

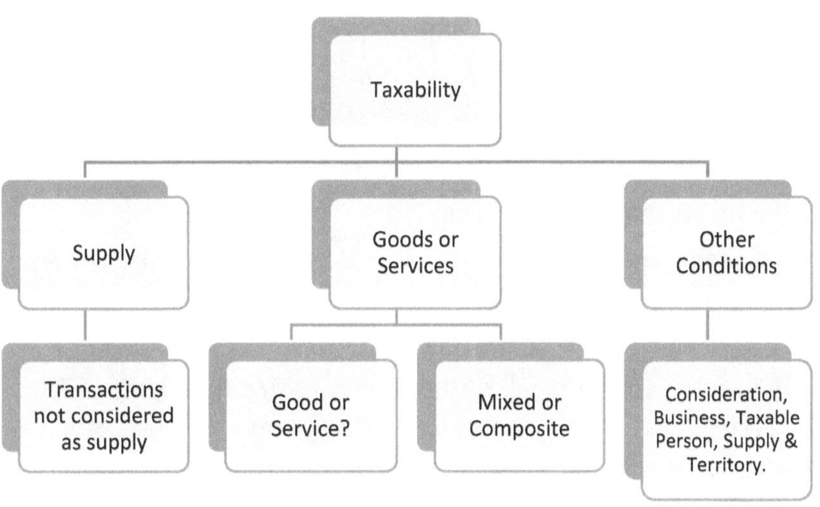

It is suggested to go through the above topics atleast twice before going forward.

<u>REGISTRATIONS</u>

Registration of business entity under the GST Law implies obtaining a unique number from the tax authorities for the purpose of collecting tax on behalf of the government and to avail Input Tax Credit for the taxes on his inward supplies. Without registration, a person can neither collect tax from his customers nor claim any Input Tax Credit of tax paid by him.

Advantages of registration to a taxpayer:

• He is legally recognized as supplier of goods or services.
• He is legally authorized to collect taxes from his customers and pass on the credit of the taxes.
• He can claim Input Tax Credit of taxes paid and can utilize the same for payment of taxes due on supply of goods or services.
• Seamless flow of Input Tax Credit from suppliers to recipients at the national level.
• Increases the credibility of the Business, thus helps in attracting more customers.

To give relief to the small businessmen a *threshold limit* of Rs **40 lakhs** has been announced for **goods** dealer. Small businesses having **all India** aggregate turnover below Rupees 40 lakh (20 lakh if business is in Arunachal Pradesh, Uttarakhand, Manipur, Mizoram, Sikkim, Meghalaya, Nagaland, Puducherry, Kerala, Telangana or Tripura) need not register. For **service provider** limit is Rs 20 lakhs for all states.

The small businesses having turnover below the threshold limit can voluntarily opt to register. But then then the liability to pay GST shall arise immediately **even if the threshold limit is not reached**.

Example – Mr Shyam has taken GST registration for his new business yet to be started. He made a first Sale of Rs 1 lakh. He think that as his sale is below threshold limit he is not liable to pay GST. This contention is wrong, once registration is taken liability starts immediately.

Further following persons are not required to take the registration:

1. Persons dealing in goods or services or both that are not liable to tax or wholly **exempt** from tax.

2. An **agriculturist**, to the extent of supply of produce out of cultivation of land.

3. Persons engaged in making supplies (selling) the tax on which is liable to be paid on **reverse charge** basis by the recipient. More detail will be discussed in Reverse charge topic.

The GST law also enlists certain categories of suppliers who are required to get **compulsory registration** irrespective of their turnover, i.e. no threshold limit shall apply. Those are listed below:

• **Inter-state** suppliers of **goods** i.e. out of State.

• A person **receiving** supplies on which tax is payable by recipient on reverse charge basis

• **Casual taxable person** who is not having fixed place of business in the State or Union Territory from where he wants to make supply.

• **Non-resident taxable persons** who are not having fixed place of business in India.

• A person who supplies on behalf of some other taxable person (i.e. an Agent of Principal)

• E-commerce operators, who provide platform to the suppliers to supply through them like Flipkart, Amazon.

• Suppliers of **goods** who supply through an e-commerce operator. Example – Person selling goods through Flipkart, Amazon.

• Notified Ecommerce operators – Housekeeping, Taxi and Hotels Services.

• TDS Deductor and Input Service Distributor.

• Those supplying online information and data base access or retrieval services from outside India to a non-registered person in India.

*In Reverse Charge mechanism the liability to pay tax rest with the **recipient** of supply of goods or services instead of the supplier. The chargeability gets reversed that is why it is called* *reverse charge. This topic has been covered in more detail in upcoming chapter.*

Examples: Are the following person liable to take GST registration?

1. A trader who is only dealing with exempt good i.e. Salt having a turnover of Rs 10 crores. **NO**

2. A farmer selling paddy to Agriculture Gramin Samiti of Rs 80 lakhs. **NO**

3. A lawyer giving his services only to a factory wherein tax is payable under reverse charge. **NO** registration is required to be taken by the lawyer.

4. A freelancer - IT engineer having turnover of Rs 15 lakhs pa is working for companies located in Bangalore, Delhi, Pune and Kolkata. **NO**

5. A freelancer - IT engineer having turnover of Rs 25 lakhs pa is working for companies located in Bangalore, Delhi, Pune and Kolkata. **YES**

6. A trader having turnover of Rs 50 lakhs pa supplying goods to customers located in Bangalore, Delhi, Pune and Kolkata. **YES**

7. A trader having turnover of Rs 5 lakhs pa supplying goods to customers located in Bangalore, Delhi, Pune and Kolkata. **YES**

8. A factory unregistered under GST having a turnover of Rs 2 lakh taking a service from lawyer. **YES** factory needs to register and pay under reverse charge.

9. Do flipkart and Amazon have to take GST registration as they are only providing platform? **YES**.

10. A person turnover of only 2 lakhs pa selling his goods from Amazon. **YES**

MULTIPLE GSTIN

Supplier has to register in **each** of such State or Union territory from where **he effects supply**. In GST registration, the supplier is allotted a 15-digit GST identification number called "GSTIN". Registration under GST is not tax specific, which means that there is single registration for all the taxes i.e. CGST, SGST/UTGST, IGST and cesses.

A legal entity would have **one GSTIN per State**, which means an entity having its branches in multiple States will have to take separate state-wise registration for the branches in each different States.

Example – SBI having branches in every state. SBI has to take separate GST registration in every state. GSTIN will be different in all the states.

Within a State, an entity with different branches would have single registration wherein it can declare one place as principal place of business and other branches as additional place of business. However, person having multiple places of business in a State may be granted a separate registration for each such place of business, if needed.

A person who has obtained or is required to obtain more than one registration, whether in one or more State shall, in respect of each such registration, be treated as **Distinct Persons** for the purposes of GST law. All separately registered business of a person shall pay tax on supply made to another registered business of such person and issue a tax invoice for such supply.

Example – SBI located in Bangalore providing services to SBI Bhopal will have to charge GST and issue tax invoice, even though both belongs to same entity SBI.

PROCEDURAL ASPECTS

An application for registration has to be submitted online within **thirty days** from the date when **liability to register** arise. The Casual and Non-Resident taxable persons need to apply at least five days prior to the commencement of the business along with the security deposit.

Documents required to get GST registration:

- PAN card and Aadhar Card
- Photo
- Business Address proof - Electricity bill and Rent agreement/NOC
- Cancelled cheque
- In case of Partnership firm - Partnership deed and KYC of all partners
- In case of LLP/Company - Incorporation Certificate and KYC of all directors

   KYC means PAN and Aadhar Card/Passport/Driving License.

The Proper Officer has to either approve the registration or raise a query within three **working** days failing which, registration would be considered as deemed to have been approved.

The registration shall be effective from the date on which the person becomes liable to registration where the application for registration has been submitted within a period of thirty days from such date; otherwise the date of the grant of registration.
This date is crucial because input tax credit can be claimed from this date.

Physical verification is to be resorted only where it is found necessary. If at all, it is felt necessary, it will be undertaken only after granting the registration, and the verification report along with the supporting documents and photographs, shall have to be uploaded on the online common portal within fifteen working days following the date of such verification.

Every registered person shall display Goods and Services Tax Identification Number on the name board and registration certificate in a prominent location at his principal place of business and at every additional place or places of business.

Amendments - In case the change is for legal name of the business, or the State of place of business or additional place of business, the taxable person will apply for amendment (change) within **15 days** of the event necessitating the change.

Cancellation - The proper officer **may** cancel the registration of a person from such date, including any retrospective date, as he may deem fit, where,—

(*a*) A registered person has violated provisions of the Act or the rules; or (*b*) A person paying tax under Composition Scheme has not furnished returns for three **consecutive** tax periods; or

(*c*) Any registered person, other than a person opted for Composition scheme, has not furnished returns for a **continuous** period of six months; or

(*d*) Any person who has taken **voluntary registration** has not **commenced** business within six months from the date of registration; or

(*e*) Registration has been obtained by means of fraud, wilful misstatement or suppression of facts; or

(f) Does not conduct any business from the declared place of business; or

(g) Issues invoice or bill without supply of goods or services. They are known as hawala dealers.

Before cancelling the registration, tax officer shall give the person an opportunity of being heard. That is to say tax officer before cancelling will issue show-cause notice to seek the explanation why his registration certificate should not be cancelled.

Example:

1. A registered person has not filed his GST return from July 2017 to December 2017.

2. A registered person has not filed his GST return from July 2017 to September 2017 and November 2017 to February 2018.

3. A registered person having a sale of around Rs 5 crores in last year does not have a single rupees sale in last 7 month, filing his GST return timely with department.

4. A voluntary registered person has not commenced his business even after 6 months of taking registration but is filing his GST return timely with department.

5. A voluntary registered person has commenced the business but unfortunately no customer walked in and the sale is zero from last eight months.

6. A registered person registered in Mumbai address but he is no more working from Mumbai. He has shifted to pune from last 4 months.

Case – 1, 4, 6 - Officer may cancel the registration.

Case – 2, 3, 5 – Officer cannot cancel the registration.

Topics Covered so far:
Advantages, Exemptions, Mandatory Registrations, Multiple GSTIN, Procedural Aspects, Amendments, Cancellation

TIME OF SUPPLY

In order to calculate and discharge tax liability, it is important to know the date on which the charging event has occurred i.e. the **date** when the tax liability arises. This event is known as Time of Supply.

The phrase "the date on which supplier receives the payment" or "the date of receipt of payment" means the date on which payment is entered in his books of accounts or the date on which the payment is credited to his bank account, whichever is earlier.

Time of issue of invoice for supply

It's important to learn about the time of issue of invoice because practically invoice is the key document which decides the time of supply.

An invoice for supply of goods needs to be issued **before or at** the time of **removal of goods** for supply to the recipient, where the supply involves **movement** of goods.

However, in other cases, an invoice needs to be issued before or at the time of **delivery** of goods or while making goods available to the recipient.

Similarly an invoice for supply of services needs to be issued **before or after** the provision of service but **not later** than thirty days from the date of provision of service (performance of services).

Time of supply of goods (Default Rule)

Earliest of the following dates:

• Date of issue of invoice by the supplier. If the invoice is not issued, then the last date on which the supplier is legally bound to issue the invoice with respect to the supply.

• Date on which the supplier receives the payment.

Example

Date of removal	Date of Invoice	Date of payment	Time of Supply
01.09.2017	01.09.2017	05.09.2017	01.09.2017
01.09.2017	01.09.2017	04.08.2017	04.08.2017
01.09.2017	03.09.2017	05.09.2017	03.09.2017
01.09.2017	Not issued	05.09.2017	01.09.2017
01.09.2017	Not issued	04.08.2017	04.08.2017

Time of supply of services (Default Rule)

• If the invoice is issued within the prescribed period - Date of issue of invoice by the supplier or the date of receipt of payment, whichever is earlier.

• If the invoice is not issued within the prescribed period - Date of provision of service or the date of receipt of payment, whichever is earlier.

Example:

Date of provision of service	Date of Invoice	Date of payment	Time of Supply
01.09.2017	01.09.2017	05.09.2017	01.09.2017
01.09.2017	01.09.2017	04.08.2017	04.08.2017
01.09.2017	03.09.2017	05.09.2017	03.09.2017
01.09.2017	03.10.2017	05.09.2017	01.09.2017
01.09.2017	28.08.2017	05.09.2017	28.08.2017
01.09.2017	28.08.2017	04.08.2017	04.08.2017
01.09.2017	Not issued	05.09.2017	01.09.2017
01.09.2017	Not issued	04.08.2017	04.08.2017

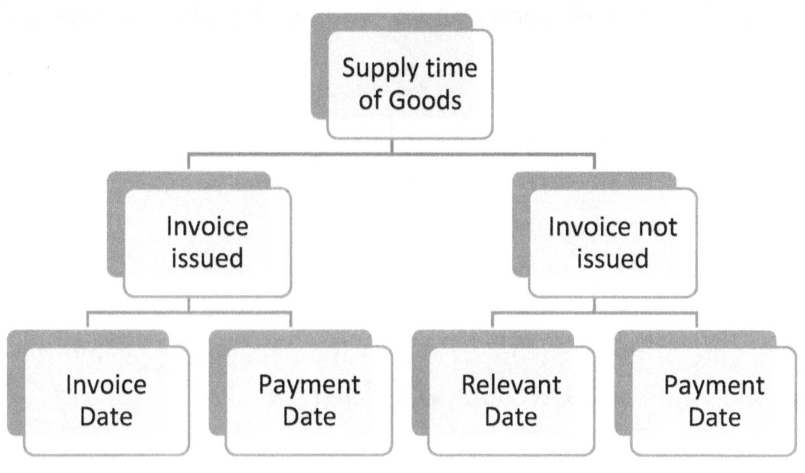

Supply time of Goods
Invoice issued
Invoice not issued
Invoice Date
Payment Date
Relevant Date
Payment Date

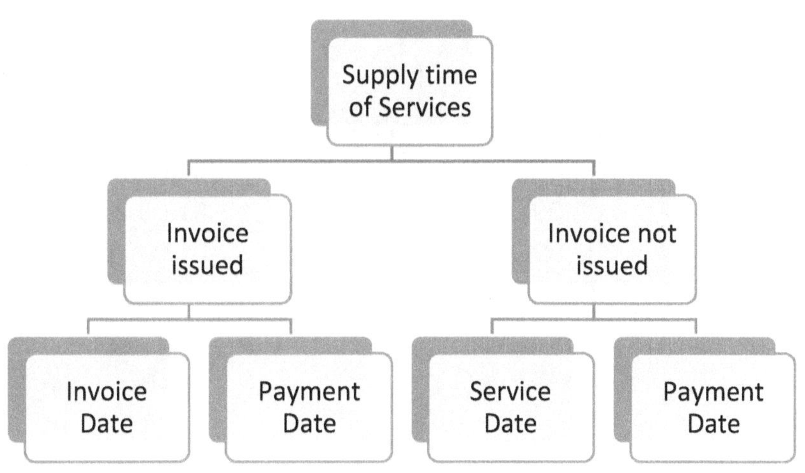

Supply time of Services
Invoice issued
Invoice not issued
Invoice Date
Payment Date
Service Date
Payment Date

Time of supply of goods when tax is to be paid on reverse charge basis

Earliest of the following dates:

• Date of receipt of goods.

• Date on which the payment is entered in the books of accounts of the recipient or the date on which the payment is debited in his bank account, whichever is earlier.

• Date immediately following **30 days** from the date of issue of invoice by the supplier.

Goods received	Payment date	Invoice date	Time of Supply
01.09.2017	01.09.2017	05.09.2017	01.09.2017
01.09.2017	03.09.2017	05.09.2017	01.09.2017
01.09.2017	03.09.2017	01.09.2017	01.09.2017
01.09.2017	03.09.2017	28.08.2017	01.09.2017
01.09.2017	27.08.2017	28.08.2017	27.08.2017

Time of supply of services when tax is to be paid on reverse charge basis

Earliest of the following dates:

• Date of payment as entered in the books of account of the **recipient** or the date on which the payment is debited in his bank account, whichever is earlier;

• Date immediately **following** 60 days from the date of issue of invoice by the **supplier**.

Date of payment in books	Date of payment in bank account	Date of Invoice	Time of Supply
01.09.2017	01.09.2017	05.09.2017	01.09.2017
01.09.2017	03.09.2017	05.09.2017	01.09.2017
04.09.2017	01.09.2017	05.09.2017	01.09.2017
02.09.2017	02.09.2017	01.09.2017	02.09.2017
02.09.2017	02.09.2017	01.07.2017	30.08.2017

VALUE OF SUPPLY

In GST, tax is payable on **ad-valorem basis** i.e. percentage of value of the supply of goods or services. Therefore, it is essential to know the value so as to ascertain the tax liability.

If the supplier & the recipient are not related and price is the sole consideration the taxable value shall be the transaction value i.e. price actually paid or payable. In most of the cases of regular normal trade, the **invoice value will be the taxable value**. In case of imported goods, value shall be determined in accordance with the provisions of section 3 of the Customs Tariff Act, 1975.

The transaction value of supply shall include——

(*a*) Taxes, fees, charges levied under any law except GST law.

(b) Expenses incurred by the recipient on behalf of the supplier.

(*c*) Incidental expenses, including **commission** and **packing**, charged by the supplier to the recipient of a supply and any amount charged for anything done by the supplier in respect of the supply of goods or services or both **at the time of** or **before** delivery of goods or supply of services.

(*d*) Interest or late fee or penalty for delayed payment of any **consideration**.

Discounts like trade discount, quantity discount etc. are part of the normal trade and commerce. Therefore, pre-supply discounts i.e. discounts **recorded in the invoice** have been allowed to be excluded while determining the taxable value.

Examples:

• Mr Parker sold the pen to Mr Writer for Rs 500/-. Transaction value will be Rs 500. Tax will be calculated on Rs 500/-

• Mr Parker sold the pen to Mr Writer for Rs 500/- at a discount of 10%. Transaction value will be Rs 450. Tax will be calculated on Rs 450 (500-10%)

• Mr Parker sold the pen pricing Rs 500 along with special packing costing Rs 100 extra. Transaction value will be Rs 600. Tax will be calculated on Rs 600 (500+100)

Taxable value when consideration is not solely in money

In such cases following values have to be taken **SEQUENTIALLY** to determine the taxable value:

i. Open Market Value of such supply.

ii. Total money value of the supply i.e. monetary consideration plus money value of the non-monetary consideration.

iii. Value of supply of like kind and quality.

iv. Value of supply based on cost i.e. cost of supply plus 10% mark-up.

v. Value of supply determined by using reasonable means consistent with principles & general provisions of GST law. (Best Judgement method)

Example: A mobile dealer gave mobile from his shop to his father for free. The open market value of mobile is Rs 25000. So, transaction Value will be taken as Rs 25000 for calculating GST.

Example: A car dealer gave a customized car from his shop to Mr Viru in exchange of iPhone X and cash 2 lakh. As the car is customized one the open market value is not available. However, it is known that iPhone price is Rs 1 lakh. So here the transaction value will be taken as Rs 3 lakhs (2 lakh + 1 lakh).

Example: A mobile dealer gave mobile from his shop to his mother for free. The cost of the mobile is Rs 20000/- and the open market value of mobile is Rs 25000. So, transaction Value will be taken as Rs 25000, as the rules have to be applied sequentially.

PLACE OF SUPPLY AND IGST

IGST tax would be levied by the Central Government on all Inter-State transactions of taxable goods or services.

It is very important to determine the place of supply – whether it is inter-State or intra-State, as the kind of tax to be paid (IGST or CGST+SGST) depends on that.

Intra State Supply means **within the State** or Union Territory.

Inter State Supply means –

• Supply of goods from one State to another State.

• Supply of services from one State to another State.

• Import of goods till they the cross customs frontier.

• Import of services.

• Export of goods or services.

• Supply of goods or services to SEZ.

• Supply of goods or services by SEZ.

• Supplies to international tourists.

• Any other supply in the taxable territory which is not intra-State supply.

PLACE OF SUPPLY

Places of supply provisions have been framed for goods and services, keeping in mind the destination/consumption principle. In other words, the place of supply is based on the place of consumption of goods or services.

As goods are tangible, the determination of their place of supply, based on the consumption principle, is not difficult. Generally, the **place of delivery** of goods becomes the place of supply. However, the services being intangible in nature, it is not easy to determine the exact place where services are acquired, enjoyed and consumed.

In respect of certain categories of services, the place of supply is determined with reference to a prescribed rules. Separate provisions for the supply of goods and services, and further in respect of domestic supplies and cross border supplies, have been made for the determination of their place of supply.

<u>**Important Note:**</u>

Intra-State supply of goods or services is when the location of the <u>supplier</u> **and** the place of supply are in same state. In an Intra-State transactions, a seller has to collect both CGST and SGST from the buyer.

Inter-State supply of goods or services is when the location of the supplier **and** the place of supply are in different states. In an Inter-State transaction, a seller has to collect only IGST from the buyer.

A. Place of supply of goods other than import and export

Nature of Supply	Place of Supply
Where the supply involves the movement of goods, whether by the supplier or the recipient or by any other person	Location of the **goods** at the time of delivery to the recipient.
Where the goods are delivered to the recipient, or any person on the direction of the third person by way of transfer of title or otherwise, it shall be deemed that the third person has received the goods	The principal place of business of such person.
Where there is no movement of goods either by supplier or recipient.	Location of such goods at the time of delivery to the recipient
Where goods are assembled or installed at site	The place where the goods are assembled or installed
Where the goods are supplied on-board a conveyance like a vessel, aircraft, train or motor vehicle	The place where such **goods** are **taken onboard**.

B. Place of supply of goods in case of Import & Export

Import	Location of Importer
Export	Location of Exporter

Example: Newton of Mumbai, Maharashtra sells ten TV sets to Vijay of Nagpur, Maharashtra.

The place of supply is Nagpur, Maharashtra. Since it is the same state CGST & SGST will be charged.

Example: Newton of Mumbai, Maharashtra sells 30 TV sets to Vinod of Bangalore, Karnataka.

The place of supply is Bangalore in Karnataka. Since it is a different state IGST will be charged.

Example: If person A in Maharashtra ships goods to Person C in Tamil Nadu on the instructions of Person B in Maharashtra, what is the place of supply?

When supplier A delivers goods to recipient C at the direction of third person B, the goods will be deemed to have been received by B and the place of supply shall be the place of B. Therefore, even if the goods were moved by A in Maharashtra to C in Tamil Nadu, it would be deemed to be received by B in Maharashtra and therefore CGST+SGST would be charged by A.

Example: Mr. Raj of Mumbai, Maharashtra gets an order of 100 TV sets from Heaven Ltd. of Chennai, Tamil Nadu. Heaven Ltd mentions that it will arrange its own transportation and take TV sets from Mr. Raj ex-factory.

In this case, Place of supply will be Maharashtra and therefore, CGST & SGST will be charged. For the reason that the goods are received ex-factory, i.e., in Maharashtra, the movement of the goods terminates for delivery to the recipient there. It is immaterial whether the receiver further transports the goods or not.

Example: Iron & Steel Ltd. (Multi state located) asks M/s SAS Constructions (West Bengal) to build a blast furnace in their Jharkhand steel plant.

Place of supply will be Jharkhand.

Example: Jay is travelling from Mumbai to Delhi by air. He purchases coffee and snacks while on the plane. The airlines is registered in both Mumbai and Delhi.

Place of supply will be Mumbai as the food items were loaded into the plane at Mumbai. So, place of supply becomes Mumbai.

Example: Ramesh is travelling to Mumbai via train. The train starts at Delhi and stops at certain stations before Mumbai. Vinod boards the train at Vadodara (Gujarat) and promptly purchases lunch on board. The lunch had been boarded in Delhi.

Place of supply will be Delhi as the food items were loaded into the train at Delhi. So, place of supply becomes Delhi.

Example: Ms. Madhuri imports school bags from China for her shop (registered in Mumbai)

Place of supply will be Mumbai.

C. Place of supply of services in case of Domestic Supplies
(Where the location of supplier of services and the location of the recipient of services is in India)

Nature of Supply	Place of Supply
Immovable property related to services, including hotel accommodation	Location at which the immovable property or boat or vessel is located or intended to be located. If located outside India: Location of the recipient.
Restaurant and catering services, personal grooming, fitness, beauty treatment and health service	Location where the services are actually performed
Training and performance appraisal	B2B: Location of such Registered Recipient B2C: Location where the services are actually performed
Admission to an event or amusement park	Place where the event is actually held or where the park or the other place is located
Organisation of an event	B2B: Location of such Registered Recipient B2C: Location where the event is actually held If the event is held outside India: Location of the recipient
Transportation of goods, including mails	B2B: Location of such Registered Person B2C: Location at which such goods are handed over for their transportation

Passenger Transportation	B2B: Location of such Registered Person B2C: Place where the passenger embarks on the conveyance for a continuous journey
Services on board a Conveyance	Location of the first scheduled point of departure of that conveyance for the journey
Banking and other financial services	Location of the recipient of services on the records of the supplier Location of the supplier of services if the location of the recipient of services is not available
Insurance services	B2B: Location of such Registered Person B2C: Location of the recipient of services on the records of the supplier
Advertisement services to the Government	The place of supply shall be taken as located in each of such States. Proportionate value in case of multiple States
Telecommunication Services	Services involving fixed line, circuits, dish etc., and place of supply is the location of such fixed equipment. In case of mobile/Internet post-paid services, it is the location of billing address of the recipient. In case of sale of pre-paid voucher, the place of supply is the place of sale of such vouchers. In other cases, it is the address of the recipient in records.

Other Services – B2B	Location of such Registered Recipient
Other Services – B2C	Location of the recipient where the address on record exists. Location of the supplier of services in other cases

Exports and supplies to SEZs are considered as 'zero rated supply' on which no tax is payable. However, ITC is allowed and refunds in respect of such supplies may be claimed.

Example: Raju Hotels in Mumbai, Maharashtra, provides catering services to Kailash Ltd. (registered in Gujarat) for their annual sales event in Mumbai.

Supply of service: Catering
Place of supply: Maharashtra
GST: CGST + SGST

Example: Jairaj (Karnataka) has been advised to take an ayurvedic treatment at Sai Ayurvedic Centre in Kerala.

Supply of service: Health Services
Place of supply: Kerala
GST: CGST + SGST

Example: Maya Industries Ltd (Gujarat) hires Source Consultancy (Mumbai) to impart soft-skills training to its employees. The training will be conducted in Mumbai.

Supply of service: Training
Place of supply: Gujarat (since the recipient is a registered person, location of recipient is the place of supply)

GST: IGST

Example: Ms. Anita (unregistered person based in Bangalore) signs up with Patro Consultancy (Mumbai) for a training on public speaking. She attends the training in Mumbai.

Supply of service: Training
Place of supply: Maharashtra (since the recipient is unregistered person, location where services are provided is the place of supply)
GST: CGST + SGST

Example: A person belonging to Karnataka buys admission tickets for Nicco Park (amusement park) in Kolkata, West Bengal from the Nicco Park organizers.

Supply of service: Admission
Place of supply: West Bengal (Location of the park)
GST: CGST+SGST

Example: First Event Managers (Mumbai) is hired by Samsung Electronics (Gujarat) to organize their annual sales event in Mumbai.

Supply of service: Event management
Place of supply: Gujarat (since the recipient is a registered person, location of recipient is the place of supply)
GST: IGST

Example: Third Event Managers (Mumbai) is hired by Ms. Malini (based in Bangalore) to manage her sister's wedding (held in Mumbai).

Supply of service: Event management

Place of supply: Mumbai (since the recipient is unregistered person, location of event is the place of supply)
GST: CGST+SGST

Example: Second Event Managers (Mumbai) is hired by Kailash Electronics Limited (Gujarat) to organize their annual business collaboration event in Singapore.

Supply of service: Event management
Place of supply: Gujarat (since the recipient is a registered person, location of recipient is the place of supply). Location of event is immaterial.
GST: IGST

Example: Jack and Jack Event Managers (Mumbai) is hired by Ms. Shalini (based in Bangalore) to manage her sister's wedding (held in Dubai).

Supply of service: Event management
Place of supply: Bangalore (since the location of event is outside India, the location of recipient is the place of supply)
GST: IGST

INPUT TAX CREDIT

Input tax credit means at the time of paying tax on output, you can reduce the tax you have already paid on inputs and pay the balance amount. Uninterrupted and seamless chain of input tax credit (hereinafter referred to as, "ITC") is one of the key features of Goods and Services Tax. ITC is a mechanism to avoid cascading of taxes.

Any registered person can avail credit of tax paid on the **inward** supply of goods or services or both, which is used or intended to be used in the course or furtherance of **business**.

Example-
Tax payable on output (Sales) is Rs 450
Tax paid on input (Purchases) is Rs 300

Input Credit of Rs 300 can be taken and only balance Rs 150 needs to be paid.

The rule to avail and utilise the credit of these taxes is as follows:

Credit of	To be utilized first for payment of	May be utilized further for payment of
CGST	CGST	IGST
SGST/UTGST	SGST/UTGST	IGST
IGST	IGST	CGST or SGST

**The pre-requisites for availing credit by registered person
are:**

a. He is in possession of **tax invoice**.

b. He has **received** the goods or services.

c. Tax is actually **paid** by the supplier.

d. He has furnished the **return**.

If the inputs are received in lots, he will be eligible to avail the
credit only when the last lot of the inputs is received.

Further, Receiver should pay the supplier, the value of the
goods or services along with the tax **within 180 days** from the
date of issue of invoice, failing which the amount of credit
availed by the recipient would be added to his output tax
liability, with interest@18% pa. This will help small business to
ensure that they receive payment within 180 days.

Where the goods or services or both are used by the
registered person partly for the purpose of any business and
partly for other purposes, the amount of credit shall be
restricted to so much of the input tax as is attributable to the
purposes of his business i.e. proportionate basis.

To avoid the misuse of credit provision, law has listed few goods and services in which credit shall not be allowed. ITC is not available in some cases as mentioned below:

a. motor vehicles and other conveyances.[1] with general insurance and repair and maintenance.

b. Goods or services provided in relation to Food and beverages, outdoor catering, beauty treatment, health services, cosmetic and plastic surgery.

c. Membership of a club, health and fitness center.

d. Rent-a-cab, life insurance and health insurance.[2]

e. **Travel benefits** extended to employees on **vacation** such as leave or home travel concession.

f. Works contract services when supplied for construction of immovable property (**other than plant & machinery**), except where it is an input service for further supply of works contract service.

g. Goods or services received by a taxable person for construction of immovable property on his own account, other than plant & machinery, even when used in course or furtherance of business.

e. Goods and/or services on which tax has been paid under **composition scheme**.

f. Goods and/or services used for private or **personal** consumption, to the extent they are so consumed.

g. Goods lost, stolen, destroyed, written off, gifted, or free samples.

So for the above inputs, no tax credit shall be allowed i.e. no benefit of GST paid can be taken.

Note:

1. Exception - when they are used—

(i) for further supply of such vehicles or conveyances; or transportation of passengers; or imparting training on driving, flying, navigating such vehicles or conveyances or sitting capacity more than thirteen;

(ii) for transportation of goods.

2. Exception - where it is obligatory for an employer under any law or such inward supply of goods or services or both of a particular category is used by a registered person for making an outward taxable supply of the same category of goods or services or both or as part of a taxable composite or mixed supply.

3. Construction includes re-construction, renovation, additions or alterations or repairs, to the extent of capitalisation, to the said immovable property.

4. Plant and machinery means apparatus, equipment, and machinery fixed to earth by foundation or structural support that are used for making outward supply of goods or services or both and includes such foundation and structural supports but excludes—
(*i*) land, building or any other civil structures;
(*ii*) telecommunication towers; and
(*iii*) pipelines laid outside the factory premises.

PAYMENT OF TAX

There are three different ledgers which need to be maintained for payment of tax.

Electronic Tax Liability Ledger

All **liabilities** of a taxable person shall be recorded and maintained in an electronic liability register. The electronic tax liability ledger would **show the tax due** from a regular tax return, and the interest, penalty, demand notice under each of the major heads.

Date	Reference no	Description	Amount debited/credited			Balance		
			IGST	SGST	CGST	IGST	SGST	CGST

Electronic Credit Ledger

All the taxes paid on the inputs would be recorded in the electronic credit ledger. Details of the **input tax credit** available under all heads would be reflected in the Electronic Credit Ledger.

IGST: The IGST input tax credit is used for payment of IGST then the remaining ITC can be used to pay tax liability under CGST or SGST. **First IGST credit has to be cleared before going forward.**

CGST: The CGST input tax credit cannot be used to pay the SGST liability but can be used to pay the liability under IGST.

SGST: The SGST input tax credit cannot be used to pay the CGST liability but can be used to pay the liability under IGST.

Electronic Cash Ledger

The taxpayer can pay the tax due through electronic modes like internet banking or by using credit/debit cards or National Electronic Fund Transfer or Real Time Gross Settlement and it will be automatically reflected to his electronic cash ledger. It is mandatory for businesses making payment for more than Rs 10,000 to do it electronically.

Payments would be made under **3 major heads** named CGST, SGST, IGST and it is further divided into the different **minor heads** like tax, interest, penalty, fees and others. The electronic cash ledger will also display the balance available under the various combination of the major-minor head.

All the payments under GST have to be made by either using the input tax credit available in the electronic credit ledger or through the electronic cash ledger. A unique identification number shall be generated at the common portal for each debit or credit to the electronic cash or credit ledger.

The amount deducted under TDS provision or the amount collected under TCS mechanism or the amount payable on reverse charge basis or the amount payable under composition scheme or any amount payable towards interest, penalty and fees shall be paid by debiting the **electronic cash ledger** only.

Every taxable person shall first discharge his tax and other dues (includes interest, penalty, fee or any other amount payable) of previous tax periods and thereafter of the current tax period.

Interest on delayed payment of GST has to be paid at the rate of **18% p.a.** and in case of excess ITC claimed / excess reduction in output tax liability by taxpayer then interest rate will be 24% p.a.

Question: Slow Associates was late in filing the return for the month of September 2017, the gst portal shows that he needs to pay the late fees of Rs 1500 under CGST and Rs 1500 under SGST. He is having sufficient balance in Electronic Credit Ledger. Can the firm utilise this balance?

Answer: No, interest, penalty or late fees has to be paid through Electronic Cash Ledger. So first the firm has to deposit the amount into Electronic Cash Ledger through the bank account and then clear the liability.

Question: KKR Ltd has not filed the August and September return. The relevant details of August is not available to file the return. But for September month he has all the related details. Can he file September month return before filing August return?

Answer: No, previous period return and liability has to be cleared before filing the current period.

Question: Following are the balances shown in the GST Electronic Ledger of Mr Mohan. Kindly guide him how the liability will be cleared.

	CGST	SGST	IGST	TOTAL
Liability Ledger	10,000	10,000	25,000	45,000
Credit Ledger	8,000	8,000	8,000	24,000
Cash Ledger	50,000	50,000	50,000	1,50,000

Answer:

Liability will be set-off in the following manner:

	CGST	SGST	IGST	TOTAL
Liability Ledger	10,000	10,000	25,000	45,000
Credit Ledger	8,000	8,000	8,000	24,000
Cash Ledger	2,000	2,000	17,000	21,000

Balance left in the Electronic Ledgers after set-off:

	CGST	SGST	IGST	TOTAL
Liability Ledger	0	0	0	0
Credit Ledger	0	0	0	0
Cash Ledger	48,000	48,000	33,000	1,29,000

Question: Following are the balances shown in the GST Electronic Ledger of Mr Raju. Kindly guide him how the liability will be cleared.

	CGST	SGST	IGST	TOTAL
Liability Ledger	10,000	10,000	25,000	45,000
Credit Ledger	18,000	18,000	8,000	44,000
Cash Ledger	50,000	50,000	50,000	1,50,000

Answer:

Liability will be set-off in the following manner:

	CGST	SGST	IGST	TOTAL
Liability Ledger	10,000	10,000	25,000	45,000
Credit Ledger	10,000	10,000	*24,000	44,000
Cash Ledger	0	0	1,000	1,000

*8,000 from IGST, 8000 CGST, 8000 SGST Credit Ledger.

Balance left in the Electronic Ledgers after set-off:

	CGST	SGST	IGST	TOTAL
Liability Ledger	0	0	0	0
Credit Ledger	0	0	0	0
Cash Ledger	50,000	50,000	49,000	1,49,000

Question: Following are the balances shown in the GST Electronic Ledger of Mr Raju. Kindly guide him how the liability will be cleared.

	CGST	SGST	IGST	TOTAL
Liability Ledger	10,000	10,000	25,000	45,000
Credit Ledger	8,000	8,000	50,000	66,000
Cash Ledger	50,000	50,000	50,000	1,50,000

Answer:

Liability will be set-off in the following manner:

	CGST	SGST	IGST	TOTAL
Liability Ledger	10,000	10,000	25,000	45,000
Credit Ledger	*10,000	~10,000	25,000	45,000
Cash Ledger	0	0	0	0

Balance left in the Electronic Ledgers after set-off:

	CGST	SGST	IGST	TOTAL
Liability Ledger	0	0	0	0
Credit Ledger	8,000	8,000	5,000	21,000
Cash Ledger	50,000	50,000	50,000	1,50,000

*10,000 from IGST Credit Ledger.
~10,000 from IGST Credit Ledger.
First IGST credit ledger has to be utilised then only we can use CGST or SGST. That means IGST credit ledger needs to be zero before using cgst or sgst credit ledgers.

Question: Following are the balances shown in the GST Electronic Ledger of Mr Ram. Kindly guide him how the liability will be cleared.

	CGST	SGST	IGST	TOTAL
Liability Ledger	10,000	10,000	25,000	45,000
Credit Ledger	8,000	8,000	26,000	42,000
Cash Ledger	50,000	50,000	50,000	1,50,000

Answer:

Liability will be set-off in the following manner:

	CGST	SGST	IGST	TOTAL
Liability Ledger	10,000	10,000	25,000	45,000
Credit Ledger	*9,000	8,000	25,000	42,000
Cash Ledger	1,000	2,000	0	3,000

Balance left in the Electronic Ledgers after set-off:

	CGST	SGST	IGST	TOTAL
Liability Ledger	0	0	0	0
Credit Ledger	0	0	0	0
Cash Ledger	49,000	48,000	50,000	1,47,000

*8,000 from CGST and 1000 from IGST Credit Ledger.

Alternatively this 1000 could also have been used for SGST liability setoff or Rs 500 in cgst and Rs 500 is sgst (any ratio). This is the new amendment, government wants that first IGST credit ledger should be made zero before utilising CGST and SGST.

Question: Following are the balances shown in the GST Electronic Ledger of Mr Dixit. Kindly guide him how the liability will be cleared.

	CGST	SGST	IGST	TOTAL
Liability Ledger	10,000	10,000	25,000	45,000
Credit Ledger	8,000	8,000	28,000	44,000
Cash Ledger	50,000	50,000	50,000	1,50,000

Answer:

Liability will be set-off in the following manner:

	CGST	SGST	IGST	TOTAL
Liability Ledger	10,000	10,000	25,000	45,000
Credit Ledger	*10,000	~9,000	25,000	44,000
Cash Ledger	0	1,000	0	1,000

Balance left in the Electronic Ledgers after set-off:

	CGST	SGST	IGST	TOTAL
Liability Ledger	0	0	0	0
Credit Ledger	0	0	0	0
Cash Ledger	50,000	49,000	50,000	1,49,000

*8,000 from CGST and 2000 from IGST Credit Ledger.
~8,000 from SGST and 1000 from IGST Credit Ledger.

Question: Following are the balances shown in the GST Electronic Ledger of Mr Babu. Kindly guide him how the liability will be cleared.

	CGST	SGST	IGST	TOTAL
Liability Ledger	10,000	10,000	25,000	45,000
Credit Ledger	11,000	8,000	25,000	44,000
Cash Ledger	50,000	50,000	50,000	1,50,000

Answer:

Liability will be set-off in the following manner:

	CGST	SGST	IGST	TOTAL
Liability Ledger	10,000	10,000	25,000	45,000
Credit Ledger	10,000	8,000	25,000	43,000
Cash Ledger	0	2,000	0	2,000

Balance left in the Electronic Ledgers after set-off:

	CGST	SGST	IGST	TOTAL
Liability Ledger	0	0	0	0
Credit Ledger	1,000	0	0	1,000
Cash Ledger	50,000	48,000	50,000	1,48,000

COMPOSITION SCHEME

The composition levy is an alternative method of levy of tax designed for small taxpayers whose aggregate turnover is up to **Rs. 1.50 crores**. The objective of composition scheme is to bring simplicity and to reduce the compliance burden for the small taxpayers. Moreover, it is **optional** and the eligible person opting to pay tax under this scheme can pay tax at a prescribed percentage of his turnover every quarter, instead of paying tax at normal rate. However, in the case of the following States, the limit of turnover is Rs. 75 lakhs - a) Arunachal Pradesh b) Assam c) Manipur d) Meghalaya e) Mizoram f) Nagaland g) Sikkim h) Tripura i) Himachal Pradesh.

The person exercising the option to pay tax under composition shall comply with the following other conditions shall mention the words "composition taxable person, not eligible to collect tax on supplies" at the top of the bill of supply issued by him and the words "composition taxable person" on every notice or signboard displayed at a prominent place at his principal place of business and at every additional place or places of business.

The option is required to be exercised prior to the commencement of the relevant financial year.

Aggregate turnover will be computed on the basis of turnover on an **all India basis** and will include value of all taxable supplies, exempt supplies and exports made by all persons with same PAN, but would exclude inward supplies under reverse charge as well as central, State/Union Territory and Integrated taxes and cess.

Question: Tisco Ltd trader of steel has five branches, sale of each branch in the preceding year was as follows:

Maharashtra – 15 lakhs pa
Karnataka – 20 lakhs pa
Orissa – 10 lakhs pa
Rajasthan – 12 lakhs pa
Gujarat – 20 lakhs pa

Can Tisco Ltd opt for composition scheme?

Answer: Yes, as the total turnover is below 1.50 crores, the company can opt for composition scheme.

Question: Jet Ltd trader of steel has five branches, sale of each branch in the preceding year was as follows:

Maharashtra – 15 lakhs pa
Assam – 20 lakhs pa
Orissa – 10 lakhs pa
Rajasthan – 22 lakhs pa
Gujarat – 20 lakhs pa

Can Jet Ltd opt for composition scheme?

Answer: No, as the total turnover is above Rs 75 lakhs, the company cannot opt for composition scheme. Limit of Rs 75 lakhs will be applicable as Assam is special category state.

Question: Mota bhai having two business whose sale last year was as follows:

Fruit business of Apple – Rs 65 lakhs
Sale of pizza bread – Rs 90 lakhs.

There is no tax on Fruit business. Can he opt for composition scheme?

Answer: No, as the aggregate turnover is more than 1.50 crores.

PAYMENT

The tax calculation under this scheme is simple - Instead of doing detailed calculation, input tax credit eligibility and using different tax rates, composition dealer can simply pay the following rate of tax on his turnover and complete compliance.

S. No.	Category of Registered person	Rate of Tax
1	Manufacturers, other than of such goods as may be notified by the Government (Ice cream, Pan Masala, Tobacco products etc.)	1% (0.5% Central tax plus 0.5% State tax) of the turnover
2	Restaurant Services	5% (2.5% Central tax plus 2.5% State tax) of the turnover
3	Traders or any other supplier eligible for composition levy	1% (0.5% Central tax plus 0.5% State tax) of the turnover

In case a person has registration in multiple states, the option to pay tax under composition scheme will have to be exercised for all States.

If any business vertical of a registered person that has been granted a separate registration becomes ineligible to pay tax under composition scheme, all other business verticals of the said person shall consequentially become ineligible to pay tax under the said section. Thus, any intimation or application for withdrawal in respect of any place of business in any State or Union territory, shall be deemed to be an intimation in respect of all other places of business registered on the same Permanent Account Number.

Question: Tata Associates has business in three state – West Bengal, Kerala and Bihar. Now the firm wants to apply for the benefit of composition scheme in Kerala branch only. Can the firm do that?

Answer: No, scheme has to be applicable across all branches in India.

EXCLUSIONS FROM COMPOSITION SCHEME

Following persons are not allowed to opt for the composition scheme:

a) Suppliers whose aggregate turnover in the preceding financial year crossed Rs. 1.50 crores.

b) A casual taxable person or a non-resident taxable person.

c) Supplier who has purchased any goods or services from unregistered supplier unless he has paid GST on such goods or services on reverse charge basis.

d) Supplier of **services**, other than restaurant service. *It is proposed Supply of services by Composition taxpayer upto Rs 5 lakh per annum will be allowed by exempting the same.*

e) Person supplying goods which are not taxable under GST law.

f) Persons making any inter-State **outward** supplies of goods.

g) Suppliers making any supply of **goods** through an electronic commerce operator who is required to collect tax at source.

h) A manufacturer of Ice cream, Pan Masala and Tobacco products.

Question: Twinkle Associates, Architect having a turnover of only Rs 25 lakhs pa. Can she opt for composition scheme?

Answer: No, composition scheme is not available to Service provider (except Restaurant Services)

Question: Tarachand & Bhagat, a famous restaurant having a turnover of Rs 80 lakhs pa. Can the firm opt for composition scheme?

Answer: Yes, Restaurant services are allowed to avail composition scheme.

Question: Bharat Ltd, Mumbai is selling goods to its customer based in Maharashtra and Gujarat. Is company eligible for composition scheme?

Answer: No, as the company is making inter-state sale.

Question: Yogi Ltd, Kanpur is buying goods from Maharashtra and selling them to its local customer. Is company eligible for composition scheme?

Answer: Yes, as the company is making inter-state purchase and not inter-state sale.

NO INPUT TAX CREDIT

A taxable person opting to pay tax under the composition scheme is out of the credit chain. So he cannot avail Input Tax Credit on his inward supplies. The composition dealer cannot collect tax paid by him on outward supplies from his customers, as a result the registered person making purchases from a taxable person paying tax under the composition scheme cannot avail credit.

Question: A composition retail trader during the month July to September 2017 had a sale of Rs 10 lakh. He also bought the goods of around 8 lakhs and paid Rs 40,000 as GST tax on purchase during the period. How much tax he needs to pay?

Answer: Trader has to pay CGST of Rs 5000 and SGST of Rs 5000. Total Rs 10000 (10 lakh x 1%) as GST. Tax paid on purchases is not relevant as under composition scheme the Input Tax Credit is not allowed.

WITHDRAWAL

The option to pay tax under composition levy would remain valid so long as conditions mentioned. The registered person can voluntarily withdraw from the composition scheme.

The option to pay tax under composition scheme lapses from the day on which his aggregate turnover during the financial year exceeds the specified limit (Rs. 1 crores/ Rs 75 lakhs). He is required to file an intimation for withdrawal from the scheme in within **seven days** from the day on which the threshold limit has been crossed.

<u>INVOICING</u>

"Tax invoice" should be issued by a registered person supplying **taxable <u>goods</u>, before or at the time** of,—

(*a*) **<u>Removal</u>** of goods for supply to the recipient, where the supply involves movement of goods; or
(*b*) **<u>Delivery</u>** of goods or making available thereof to the recipient, in any other case.

A registered person supplying **taxable <u>services</u>** shall, before or after the provision of service but within a period of **thirty days** from the date of the supply of service, issue a Tax Invoice.

Where the goods being sent or taken on approval for sale or return are removed before the supply takes place, the invoice shall be issued before or at the time of supply or **six months** from the date of removal, whichever is earlier.

A registered person supplying exempted goods or services or both or paying tax under composition scheme, instead of a tax invoice, shall issue a **Bill of Supply**.

Registered person may not issue a tax invoice or bill of supply, if the value of the goods or services or both supplied is less than two hundred rupees and **can choose** to issue a consolidated tax invoice for such supplies at the close of **each day** in respect of all such supplies, provided the recipient is not a registered person and does not require such invoice.

Where a registered person is supplying taxable as well as exempted goods or services or both to an unregistered person, a single "invoice-cum-bill of supply" may be issued for all such supplies.

A registered person who is liable to pay tax under Reverse charge shall issue a **Payment Voucher** at the time of making payment to the supplier.

A registered person shall, on receipt of advance payment with respect to any supply of goods or services or both, issue a **Receipt Voucher**, evidencing receipt of such payment. *To facilitate trade, GST council has exempted all taxpayers from payment of tax on advances received in case of supply of goods.*

Where, on receipt of advance payment with respect to any supply of goods or services the registered person issues a receipt voucher, but subsequently no supply is made and no tax invoice is issued, the said registered person may issue to the person who had made the payment, a **Refund Voucher** against such payment.

Credit Note - Where a tax invoice has been issued for supply of any goods or services and the taxable value or tax charged in that tax invoice is found to exceed the taxable value or tax payable in respect of such supply, or where the goods supplied are returned by the recipient, or where goods or services supplied are found to be deficient, the registered person, who has supplied may issue to the recipient a credit note.

Debit Note - Where a tax invoice has been issued for supply of any goods or services and the taxable value or tax charged in that tax invoice is found to be less than the taxable value or tax payable in respect of such supply, the supplier shall issue to the recipient a debit note.

TAX INVOICE

The minimum details to be contained in the Tax Invoice are listed below:

(a) Name, address and GSTIN of the supplier

(b) Consecutive serial number not exceeding sixteen characters, in one or multiple series, containing alphabets or numerals or special characters as **"-" and "/"** respectively, and any combination thereof, unique for a financial year

(c) Date of its issue

(d) Name, address and GSTIN or UIN, if registered, of the recipient

(e) Name and address of the recipient and the address of delivery, along with the name of State and its code

(f) HSN code of goods or Accounting Code of services

(g) Description of goods or services

(h) Quantity in case of goods

(i) Total value of supply of goods or services or both

(j) Taxable value of supply of goods or services or both taking into account discount or abatement, if any

(k) **Rate** of tax (central tax, State tax, integrated tax, Union territory tax or cess)

(l) **Amount** of tax charged in respect of taxable goods or services (central tax, State tax, integrated tax, Union territory tax or cess)

(m) Place of supply along with the name of State, in case of a supply in the course of inter-State trade or commerce

(n) Address of delivery where the same is different from the place of supply

(o) Whether the tax is payable on reverse charge basis

(p) **Signature or digital signature** of the supplier or his authorized representative

The tax invoice shall be prepared in **triplicate**, in the case of supply of **goods**, in the following manner, namely,-

(a) the original copy being marked as ORIGINAL FOR RECIPIENT;

(b) the duplicate copy being marked as DUPLICATE FOR TRANSPORTER; and

(c) the triplicate copy being marked as TRIPLICATE FOR SUPPLIER.

The tax invoice shall be prepared in **duplicate**, in the case of the supply of **services**, in the following manner, namely,-

(a) the original copy being marked as ORIGINAL FOR RECIPIENT;

(b) the duplicate copy being marked as DUPLICATE FOR SUPPLIER.

Where the supplier of taxable service is a **goods transport agency** supplying services in relation to transportation of goods by road in a goods carriage, the said supplier shall issue a tax invoice containing the above listed details along with the gross weight of the consignment, name of the consigner and the consignee, registration number of goods carriage in which the goods are transported, details of goods transported, details of place of origin and destination, Goods and Services Tax Identification Number of the person liable for paying tax whether as consigner, consignee or goods transport agency.

Rules regarding mentioning **HSN code** (Harmonized System of Nomenclature) in a tax invoice involving intra-state or inter-state supply is listed below:

Annual Turnover in the **preceding** Financial Year	Number of Digits of HSN Code
Upto Rupees One Crore Fifty Lakhs	Nil
More than Rupees One Crore Fifty Lakhs and upto Rupees Five Crores	2
More than Rupees Five Crores	4

HSN code number is widely used in many countries to classify goods for taxation purpose, claiming benefits etc.

Challan or Transportation of goods without issue of invoice –

For the purposes of:

(a) supply of liquid gas where the quantity at the time of removal from the place of business of the supplier is not known,

(b) transportation of goods for job work

(c) transportation of goods for reasons other than by way of supply

the consigner may issue a **delivery challan** in lieu of invoice at the time of removal of goods for transportation, containing the following details, namely:-

(i) Date and number of the delivery challan

(ii) Name, address and GSTIN of the consigner and consignee

(iii) HSN code and description of goods

(iv) Quantity and Taxable value

(v) Tax rate and tax amount

(vi) Place of supply

(vii) Signature.

This delivery challan shall be prepared in triplicate.

ACCOUNTS AND RECORDS

The compliance verification is done by the department through scrutiny of returns, audit and/or investigation. This compliance verification can be done through documentary checks this requires taxpayer for keeping and maintaining accounts and records.

Every registered person shall keep and maintain all records at his principal place of business as mentioned in the **certificate of registration**. In case more than one place of business is specified in the certificate of registration, the accounts relating to each place of business shall be kept at such places of business.

Following accounts and records will have to be maintained by every registered person:

(a) Detailed accounts of **stock** in respect of goods received and supplied; containing particulars of the opening balance, receipt, supply, goods lost, stolen, destroyed, written off or disposed of by way of gift or free samples and balance of stock including raw materials, finished goods, scrap and wastage thereof.

(b) A separate account of **advances** received, paid and adjustments made thereto. *To facilitate trade, GST council has exempted all taxpayers from payment of tax on advances received in case of supply of goods.*

(c) Account containing the details of **tax** payable, tax collected and paid, input tax, **input tax credit** claimed together with a register of tax invoice, credit note, debit note, delivery challan issued or received during any tax period.

(d) Name and **complete** addresses of suppliers from whom goods or services chargeable to tax have been received.

(e) Name and **complete** addresses of the persons to whom supplies have been made.

(f) The complete addresses of the **premises** where the goods are stored including goods stored during transit along with the particulars of the stock stored therein.

(g) **Monthly** production accounts showing the **quantitative** details of raw materials or services used in the manufacture and quantitative details of the goods so manufactured including the waste and by products thereof.

(h) Accounts showing the quantitative details of goods used in the provision of services, details of input services utilised and the services supplied.

Every **Agent** shall maintain particulars of authorisation received by him from every principal and keep separately accounts of transaction for each principal.

Every owner or operator of warehouse or godown or any other place used for storage of goods and every transporter, irrespective of whether he is a registered person or not, shall maintain records of the consigner, consignee and other relevant details of the goods. The goods shall be stored in such manner that they can be identified item wise and owner wise and shall facilitate any physical verification or inspection, if required at any time by tax officer.

Every person engaged in the business of transporting goods shall maintain records of goods transported, delivered and goods stored in transit by him along with the Goods and Services Tax Identification Number of the registered consigner and consignee for each of his branches.

A registered person may keep and maintain such accounts and other particulars in **electronic form**. The data so stored shall be authenticated by way of digital signature.

The following additional requirements have been prescribed for maintenance of records in electronic form:

(a) Proper electronic **back-up** of records shall be maintained and preserved in such manner that, in the event of destruction of such records due to accidents or natural causes, the information can be restored within a reasonable period of time.

(b) The registered person maintaining electronic records shall produce, on demand, the relevant records or documents, duly authenticated by him, in **hard copy** or in any electronically readable format.

(c) Where the accounts and records are stored electronically by any registered person, he shall, on demand, provide the details of such files, **passwords** of such files and explanation for codes used, where necessary, **for access** and any other information which is required for such access along with a sample copy in print form of the information stored in such files.

All accounts maintained together with all invoices, bills of supply, credit and debit notes, and delivery challans relating to stocks, deliveries, inward supply and outward supply shall be preserved for **seventy two months** (six years) from the **due date** of furnishing of annual return for the year pertaining to such accounts and records and shall be kept at every related place of business mentioned in the certificate of registration.

REVERSE CHARGE MECHANISM

Reverse Charge means the liability to pay tax by the **recipient** of supply of goods or services instead of the supplier. The chargeability gets reversed that is why it is called reverse charge. It removes the burden of tax compliance from individuals with limited resources to large organisations with sufficient resources.

All persons who are required to pay tax under reverse charge have to register for GST **irrespective** of the turnover.

Recipient of supply has to issue invoice on himself. Tax under reverse charge to be paid using **Electronic Cash Ledger**. Tax paid on reverse charge basis will be available as input tax credit if such goods or services are intended to be used for business.

Two categories of reverse charge has been prescribed:

1) The GST in respect of the supply of taxable goods or services or both by **unregistered** supplier **to** a **registered** person shall be paid by such registered person on reverse charge basis as the recipient. *However, due to practical implementation difficulty this provision has been deferred till 01.04.2018.*

2) Following categories of Intra-State or Inter-State supply of goods will attract reverse charge mechanism:

Description of supply of Goods	Supplier of goods	Recipient of supply
Cashew nuts, not shelled or peeled	Agriculturist	Any registered person
Bidi wrapper leaves (tendu)	Agriculturist	Any registered person
Tobacco leaves	Agriculturist	Any registered person
Silk yarn	Any person who manufactures silk yarn from raw silk or silk worm cocoons for supply of silk yarn	Any registered person
Supply of lottery.	State Government, Union Territory or any local authority	Lottery distributor or selling agent.
Used vehicles, seized and confiscated goods, old and used goods, waste and scrap	Central Government, State Government, Union territory or a local authority	Any registered person

Following Category of Services attract reverse charge:

Description of supply of service	Supplier of service	Recipient of service
GTA Services	Goods Transport Agency (GTA)	Any factory, society, body corporate, partnership firm, casual taxable person; located in the taxable territory
Legal Services by advocate	An individual advocate, including a senior advocate or a firm of advocates	Any business entity located in the taxable territory
Services supplied by an arbitral tribunal to a business entity	An arbitral tribunal	Any business entity located in the taxable territory
Services provided by way of sponsorship to any body corporate or partnership firm.	Any person	Any body corporate or partnership firm located in the taxable territory
Services supplied by a director of a company or a body corporate.	A director of a company or a body corporate	The company or a body corporate located in the taxable territory
Services supplied by an insurance agent to any person carrying on insurance business.	An insurance agent	Any person carrying on insurance business, located in the taxable territory

Services supplied by a recovery agent to a banking company or a financial institution or a NBFC	A recovery agent	A banking company or a financial institution or a nonbanking financial company, located in the taxable territory
Supply of services by an author, music composer, photographer, artist or the like by way of transfer or permitting the use or enjoyment of a copyright.	Author or music composer, photograph her, artist, or the like	Publisher, music company, producer or the like, located in the taxable territory
Services supplied by a person located in non- taxable territory by way of transportation of goods by a vessel from a place outside India up to the customs station of clearance in India.	A person located in non-taxable territory	Importer located in the taxable territory.
Any service supplied by any person who is located in a non-taxable territory to any person other than non-taxable online recipient.	Any person located in non-taxable territory	Any person located in the taxable territory other than non-taxable online recipient.
Security Services	Any person other than a	A registered person located in taxable

	body corporate	territory.
Renting of any motor vehicle designed to carry passengers	Any person, other than a body corporate who supplies the service to a body corporate without charging GST	Any body corporate located in the taxable territory.

The person who pays or is liable to pay freight for the transportation of goods by road in goods carriage, located in the taxable territory shall be treated as the person who receives the service for the purpose of this notification.

Also Reverse charge mechanism is applicable on Services supplied by the Central Government, State Government, Union territory or local authority to a **business entity** excluding: -

(1) Renting of immovable property

(2) Services by the Department of Posts by way of speed post, express parcel post, life insurance, and agency services

(3) Services in relation to an aircraft or a vessel, inside or outside the precincts of a port or an airport

(4) Transport of goods or passengers

Further following categories of services, the tax on intra-state or inter-state supplies shall be paid by the **electronic commerce operator** –

(i) Services by way of transportation of passengers by a radio-taxi, **motorcab**, maxicab and motor cycle;

(ii) services by way of providing **accommodation** in hotels, inns, guest houses, clubs, campsites or other commercial places meant for residential or lodging purposes and **housekeeping** services except where the person supplying such service through electronic commerce operator is liable for registration.

<u>TAX DEDUCTED AT SOURCE</u>

TDS is one of the modes/methods to collect tax, under which, certain percentage of amount is deducted by a recipient at the time of making payment to the supplier.

The purpose of TDS to enable the Government to have a trail of transactions and to monitor and verify the compliances. It acts as a powerful instrument to prevent tax evasion and expands the tax net.

A TDS deductor has to compulsorily register without any threshold limit. The following persons (the deductor) are required to deduct tax at source:

(a) A department or an establishment of the Central Government or State Government

(b) Local authority

(c) Governmental agencies

The tax would be deducted @1% of the payment made to the supplier (the deductee) of taxable goods or services or both, where the total value of such supply under a **contract**, exceeds two lakh fifty thousand rupees (excluding the GST tax). Thus, individual supplies may be less than Rs. 2,50,000/-, but if contract value is more than Rs. 2,50,000/-, TDS will have to be deducted. For the purpose of deduction of tax specified above, the value of supply shall be taken as the amount excluding GST tax indicated in the invoice.

The TDS so deposited in the Government account shall be reflected in the **electronic cash ledger** of the supplier (i.e. deductee)

The amount of tax deducted at source should be deposited to the Government account and return should be filed by the deductor by 10th of the succeeding month.

A **TDS certificate** is required to be issued by deductor (the person who is deducting tax) to the deductee (the supplier from whose payment TDS is deducted), within 5 days of crediting the amount to the Government.

Example: Local Authority needs to pay Rs 5 lakhs to a contractor. The Local Authority will deduct 1% i.e. Rs 5000 and pay the balance amount Rs 495000 to the contractor. This Rs 5000 will be deposited to the GST tax department by the Local Authority.

TAX COLLECTED AT SOURCE

TCS refers to the tax which is collected by the **electronic commerce operator** when a supplier supplies some goods or services through its portal and the payment for that supply is collected by the electronic commerce operator.

Electronic commerce means the supply of goods or services or both, including digital products over digital or electronic network. Electronic commerce operator means any person who owns, operates or manages digital or electronic facility or platform for electronic commerce.

There are many e-Commerce operators [hereinafter referred to as an Operator], like Amazon, Flipkart, Jabong, etc. operating in India. These operators display on their portal products as well as services which are actually supplied by some other person to the consumer. The goods or services belonging to other suppliers are displayed on the portals of the operators and consumers buy such goods through these portals. On placing the order for a particular product, the actual supplier supplies the selected product to the consumer. The price/consideration for the product is collected by the Operator from the consumer and passed on to the actual supplier after the deduction of commission by the Operator. The Government has placed the responsibility on the Operator to collect the tax at a rate of **1%** from the supplier on the taxable supplies. This shall be done by the Operator by paying the supplier, the price of the product, less the tax, calculated at the rate of 1%.

The e-Commerce Operator need to **compulsorily register** under GST. The threshold limit of Rs. 20 lakhs (Rs. 10 lakhs for special category states) is not applicable to them.

The amount of tax collected by the Operator is required to be deposited by the 10th of the following month along with the return. The Operator is also required to file an Annual statement in prescribed form by the 31st of December following the end of every financial year.

The tax collected by the Operator shall be credited to the electronic cash ledger of the supplier who has supplied the goods/services through the Operator.

Further, tax officer have been given power to issue Notice to an Operator, asking him to furnish details relating to volume of the goods/services supplied, stock of goods lying in warehouses etc. The Operator is required to furnish such details within 15 working days.

Question: Simran is selling Mobiles through Flipkart. During the month one Mobile of Rs 20,000 was sold through the flipkart.

Answer:

Gross Sales	20000.00
TCS @ 1%	200.00
Amount payable to Simran by Flipkart	**19800.00**

Note: Simran will get the credit of Rs 200 and this will be reflected in her Electronic Cash Ledger of GST online portal.

GST RETURNS

The basic features of the returns mechanism in GST include electronic filing of returns, uploading of invoice level information and auto-population of information relating to Input Tax Credit (ITC) from returns of supplier to that of recipient, invoice-level information matching and auto-reversal of Input Tax Credit in case of mismatch.

Under GST, a regular taxpayer needs to furnish monthly returns and one annual return.

Summary of various important returns has been detailed below:

Return	Description	Filer	Due date of filing
GSTR-1	Monthly Statement of Outward supplies	Registered Person	10th of the next month
GSTR-2	Monthly Statement of Inward supplies	Registered Person	15th of the next month
GSTR-3	Monthly Return for a normal taxpayer	Registered Person	20th of the next month
GSTR-4	Quarterly Return	Composition Dealer	18th of the month

			succeeding the quarter
GSTR-5	Monthly Return for a non-resident taxpayer	Non-resident Taxpayer	20th of the month succeeding the tax period & within 7 days after expiry of registration
GSTR-6	Monthly Return for an Input Service Distributor (ISD)	Input Service Distributor	13th of the next month
GSTR-7	Monthly Return for authorities deducting TDS	Tax Deductor	10th of the next month
GSTR-8	Monthly Statement for E-Commerce Operator depicting supplies effecting through it	E-Commerce Operator	10th of the next month

GSTR-9/9A/9B/9C	Annual Return	Registered Person	31st December of next Financial Year
GSTR-10	Final Return	Taxable Person whose registration has been surrendered or cancelled	Within three months of the date of cancellation or date of order of cancellation, whichever is later

Taxes has to be paid before filing of the returns.

Every registered person who is required to furnish a return GSTR 3 or GSTR 4 shall furnish such return for every tax period whether or not any supplies of goods or services or both have been made during such tax period. That is to say, even **Nil return has to be filed** by the registered person.

A registered person shall not be allowed to furnish a return for a tax period if the return for any of the previous tax periods has not been furnished by him. Any registered person who fails to furnish Return (except Form GSTR 3B) within the due dates, shall be liable to pay a late fee of Rs. 200 per day, subject to a maximum of Rs. 10,000.

The mechanism of filing revised returns for any correction of errors/omissions has been done away with. The rectification of errors/omissions is allowed in the subsequent returns.

However, no rectification is allowed after furnishing the return for the month of September following the end of the financial year to which, such details pertain, or furnishing of the relevant annual return, whichever is earlier.

The details of every inward supply furnished by the taxable person (i.e. recipient) shall be matched with the corresponding details of outward supply furnished by the corresponding taxable person (supplier) in his valid return. A return may be considered to be a valid return only when the appropriate GST has been paid **in full** by the taxable person, as shown in such return for a given tax period.

In case the details match, then the ITC claimed by the recipient in his valid returns shall be considered as finally accepted and such acceptance shall be communicated to the recipient. **Failure to file valid return by the supplier may lead to denial of ITC in the hands of the recipient.** This auto check mechanism of ITC will make the recipient not to deal further with non-complied supplier under GST law, as he has already paid the tax amount to supplier but not got the benefit of GST tax.

Every registered taxable person whose turnover during a financial year exceeds the turnover limit is above Rs 5 crores shall get his accounts audited by a Chartered Accountant or a Cost Accountant.

Note: *As the GST IT infrastructure is insufficient and due to new law challenges, changes relating to returns are happening very frequently. The due dates mentioned above might not be fully applicable. Further an additional monthly summary return in Form GSTR 3B needs to be filed every month. This GSTR 3B has replaced the relevance of GSTR 3.*

Further, government is planning to scrap this all returns and bring in place the new returns format

JOB-WORK

Job-work is any treatment or process undertaken by a person on goods belonging to another registered person. The one who does the said job would be termed as Job-worker. The ownership of the goods does not transfer to the job-worker but it rests with the principal (a person supplying taxable goods to the job-worker). The job-worker is required to carry out the process specified by the principal on the goods.

The GST Act makes special provisions with regard to removal of goods for job-work and receiving back the goods after processing from the job-worker without the payment of GST. The benefit of these provisions shall be available both to the principal and the job-worker. Principal shall be entitled to take the credit of input tax paid on inputs sent to the job-worker for the job-work.

The responsibility for keeping proper accounts for the inputs or capital goods shall lie with the principal.

Certain facilities with certain conditions are offered in relation to job-work, which are as under:

a) A registered person (Principal) can send inputs (including intermediate goods) or capital goods under intimation without payment of tax to a job-worker and from there to another job-worker and after completion of job-work bring back such goods without payment of tax. The principal is not required to reverse the ITC availed on inputs or capital goods dispatched to job-worker.

The inputs or capital goods shall be sent to the job-worker under the cover of a challan issued by the principal. The challan shall be issued even for the inputs or capital goods sent directly to the job-worker.

b) Principal can send inputs or capital goods directly to the job-worker without bringing them to his premises and can still avail the credit of tax paid on such inputs or capital goods.

c) Inputs or capital goods sent to a job-worker are required to be returned to the principal within 1 year and 3 years, respectively, from the date of sending such goods to the job-worker. If the same is not returned within the time limit then it shall be deemed that such inputs had been supplied by the principal to the job worker on the day when the said inputs were sent out. However, the provision of return of goods is not applicable in case of moulds and dies, jigs and fixtures or tools supplied by the principal to job-worker.

d) After processing of goods, the job-worker may clear the goods to-

(i) Another job-worker for further processing
(ii) Dispatch the goods to any of the place of business of the principal without payment of tax

(iii) Remove the goods on payment of tax within India or without payment of tax for export outside India on fulfilment of conditions.

The facility of supply of goods by the principal to the third party directly from the premises of the job-worker on payment of tax in India and likewise with or without payment of tax for export may be availed by the principal on declaring premise of the job-worker as his additional place of business in registration.

e) Waste generated at the premises of the job-worker may be supplied directly by the registered job-worker from his place of business on payment of tax or such waste may be cleared by the principal, in case the job-worker is not registered.

REFUNDS

Timely refund mechanism is essential in tax administration, as it facilitates trade through the release of blocked funds for working capital, expansion and modernisation of existing business. Under the GST regime, there will be a standardized form for making any claim for refunds. The claim and sanctioning procedure is online and time bound. Interest on withheld refund has to be paid at the rate of 6%. Further, Interest on delayed refund (beyond 60 days, arising from order of authority/ court) at 9% p.a.

A claim for refund may arise on account of:

1. Export of goods or services.

2. Supplies to SEZs units and developers.

3. Deemed exports. Eg – Supply of goods to EOU.

4. Refund of taxes on purchase made by UN or embassies etc.

5. Refund arising on account of judgment, decree, order or direction of the Appellate Authority, Appellate Tribunal or any court.

6. Refund of accumulated Input Tax Credit on account of inverted duty structure other than Nil rated or fully exempt supplies.

7. Finalisation of provisional assessment.

8. Refund of pre-deposit.

9. Excess payment due to mistake.

10. Refunds to International tourists of GST paid on goods in India and carried abroad at the time of their departure from India.

11. Refund on account of issuance of refund vouchers for taxes paid on advances against which, goods or services have not been supplied.

12. Refund of CGST & SGST paid by treating the supply as intra-State supply which is subsequently held as inter-State supply and vice versa.

The GST law requires that every claim for refund is to be filed within 2 years from the **relevant date**. The claim, if in order, has to be sanctioned within a period of 60 days from the date of receipt of the claim.

One of the major categories under which, claim for refund may arise would be, on account of exports. All exports (whether of goods or services) as well as supplies to SEZs have been categorised as **Zero Rated Supplies** in the IGST Act.

The applicant needs to file elaborate documents along with the refund claim. For every claim, the main document prescribed is a statement of relevant **invoices** pertaining to the claim.

A statement containing the number and date of **shipping bills** or bills of export and the number and the date of the relevant export invoices, in a case where the refund is on account of export of goods.

In case refund is on account of export of services, apart from the statement of invoices, the relevant bank realisation certificates evidencing receipt of payment in **foreign currency** is also required to be submitted.

No refund of unutilised input tax credit shall be allowed of Central tax and Integrated tax, in case of supply of services for Construction of a complex, building, civil structure or a part thereof, including a complex or building intended for sale to a buyer, wholly or partly.

PENALTY

An offender not paying tax or making short-payments has to pay a penalty of 10% of the tax amount due subject to a minimum of Rs.10,000. In case of fraud or any wilful misstatement or suppression of facts to evade tax, offender has to pay a penalty amount of tax evaded/short deducted etc., i.e., **100%** penalty, subject to a minimum of Rs. 10,000.

In case of non-compliance of TDS or TCS provision, penalty shall be amount equivalent to the tax not deducted or short deducted or deducted but not paid to the Government or tax not collected or short collected or collected but not paid to the Government, subject to a minimum of Rs. 10,000.

Further a penalty of Rs 25000 has been prescribed for any person who-

- Helps any other person to commit fraud under GST

- Acquires/receives any goods/services with full knowledge that it is in violation of GST rules

- Fails to appear before the tax authority on receiving a summons

- Fails to issue an invoice according to GST rules

- Fails to account/vouch any invoice appearing in the books

There will not be any penalty for minor breaches (tax amount is less than Rs.5000) or errors which are easily rectifiable and clearly made without any motive of fraud.

For any offence committed by a company, **both** the **officer in charge** (such as director, manager, secretary) as well as the **company** will be held liable. For LLPs, HUFs, trust, the partner/karta/managing trustee will be held liable.

Any person who supplies or receives any goods in contravention of any of the provisions of GST law, then all goods shall be liable to **confiscation**.

ASSESSMENTS

Every registered taxable person under GST shall himself assess the taxes payable and furnish a return for each tax period. The proper officer can scrutinize the return to verify its correctness. Scrutiny of returns is not a legal or judicial proceeding, i.e. no order can be passed. The officer will ask for explanations on discrepancies noticed. If the officer finds the explanation satisfactory then the taxable person will be informed and no further action will be taken. (**Self Assessment**)

The proper officer will take action if the taxable person does not give a satisfactory explanation within 30 days or does not rectify the discrepancies within a reasonable time.

The officer may-

- Conduct audit by the tax department

- Proceed for Special Audit procedure

- Inspect and Search the places of business of the tax payer

- Proceed for Demand and Recovery provisions

When the assessing officer has **sufficient grounds to believe** any delay in assessing a tax liability can harm the interest of the revenue. To protect the interest of the revenue, he can pass the summary assessment on the basis of evidence of tax liability with the prior permission of Additional/Joint commissioner.

Summary Assessment means a fast-track assessment based on the return filed by the assessee. It is completed on a priority basis without the presence of the taxpayer because the delay in such assessments may lead to loss of revenue. Summary assessment is usually done in cases of defaulting or absconding taxpayers.

In case if a registered taxable person does not file his return (even with a notice), the proper officer will assess the tax liability to the **best of his judgement.** He will assess on the basis of the available information.

Rectification - Any authority, who has passed or issued any decision or order or notice or certificate, may rectify any error which is **apparent on the face of record** in such decision or order or notice or certificate, either on its **own motion** or where such error is **brought to its notice**, within a period of **three months** from the date of issue of such decision or order or notice or certificate.

APPEAL

Any appeal under any law is an application to a higher authority/court for a reversal of the decision of a lower authority/court.

A person unsatisfied with any decision or order passed against him under GST by an adjudicating authority/tax officer can appeal to the First Appellate Authority. If he is not satisfied with the decision of the First Appellate Authority he can appeal to the Appellate Tribunal, then to High Court, and finally Supreme Court.

First appeal to **Appellate Authority** against decision or order of an adjudicating authority be filed within three months from the date on which the said decision or order is **communicated** to him. The Appellate Authority may, allow it to be presented within a further period of one month.

Appeal shall be filed by the appellant when he has paid **in full**, such part of the amount of tax, interest, fine, fee and penalty arising from the impugned order, as is **admitted** by him; and a sum equal to **ten per cent** of the remaining amount of **tax in dispute** arising from the said order, in relation to which the appeal has been filed. The recovery proceedings for the **balance amount** shall be **deemed to be stayed**.

The Appellate Authority may, at the time of hearing of an appeal, allow an appellant to add any ground of appeal not specified in the grounds of appeal. **Adjournment shall be limited to three times to a party during hearing of the appeal**. The Appellate Authority shall not refer the case back to the adjudicating authority that passed the said decision or order.

Second appeal can be filed to **Appellate Tribunal** whose powers shall be exercisable by the National Bench and Regional Benches, State Bench and Area Benches. Appeal to the Appellate Tribunal can be made within three months from the date on which the order sought to be appealed against is communicated to the person preferring the appeal. Appellate Tribunal shall have the same powers as are vested in a civil court under the Code of Civil Procedure. Appeal shall be filed after paying a sum equal to **twenty percent** of the remaining amount of tax in dispute, in addition to the amount paid during first appeal.

Any person aggrieved by any order passed by the State Bench or Area Benches of the Appellate Tribunal may file an appeal to the High Court if it involves a substantial question of law. An appeal should be filed within a period of one hundred and eighty days from the date on which the order appealed against is received by the aggrieved person.

An appeal shall lie to the Supreme Court from any order passed by the National Bench or Regional Benches of the Appellate Tribunal or from any judgment or order passed by the High Court.

All sums due to the Government under order passed by the Appellate Tribunal or passed by the High Court need to be paid even if appealed to Supreme Court.

No appeal can be filed if such order passed relates to an order pertaining to the seizure or retention of books of account, register and other documents or an order sanctioning prosecution.

<u>**DEMAND AND RECOVERY**</u>

If the assessee pays the tax on self-assessment correctly then there will not be any problem. If there is any short payment or wrong utilisation of input credit, then the GST authorities will initiate demand and recovery provisions against the assessee.

In non-fraud cases (where there is no motive to evade tax) when tax is unpaid/short paid or refund is wrongly made or input tax credit has been wrongly availed/utilized; the proper officer (GST authorities) will serve a show cause notice on the taxpayer. The maximum time limit for the order of payment is **3 years** from the **due date** for filing of annual return for the year to which the amount relates.

In tax evasion cases involving fraud, wilful misstatement or suppression of facts which results in unpaid/short paid tax or wrong refunds or wrongly availed/utilized input tax credit; in such cases, the proper officer will serve a show cause notice to the taxpayer. They will be required to pay the amount due along with interest and penalty. The maximum time limit is **5 years** from the due date for filing of annual return for the year to which the amount relates.

INSPECTION, SEARCH, SEIZURE AND ARREST

These provisions are to safeguard Government's legitimate dues. These provisions by checking evasion provide a level playing field to genuine tax payers.

'Inspection' is relatively a softer provision which enables officers to access any place of business or of a person engaged in transporting goods or who is an owner or an operator of a warehouse or godown. Inspection can also be done of the conveyance, carrying a consignment. The person in charge of the conveyance has to produce documents/devices for verification and allow inspection.

A relevant officer can do inspection only if he has **reasons to believe** that the person concerned has done one of the following actions:

(a) Suppression of any transaction relating to supply of goods or services or stock in hand.

(b) Claimed excess input tax credit.

(c) Contravention of any provisions of the Act or the Rules to evade tax.

(d) Transporting or keeping goods which escaped payment of tax or manipulating accounts or stocks which may cause evasion of tax.

Any consignment, value of which, is exceeding Rs. 50,000/- may be stopped at any place for verification of the documents/devices prescribed for movement of such consignments. If on verification of the consignment, during transit, it is found that the goods were removed without prescribed document or the same are being supplied in contravention of any provisions of the Act then the same can be detained or seized and may be subjected to penalties as prescribed.

The provisions of **search and seizure** provides that search of any place of business etc. can be carried out from a relevant officer if he has a reason to believe that the person concerned has done at least one of the following:-

(a) Goods liable to confiscation or any documents/books/record/things, which may be useful for or relevant to any proceedings, are secreted in any place then all such places can be searched.

(b) All such goods/documents/books/record/things may be seized, however, if it is not practicable to seize any such goods then the same may be detained. The person from whom these are seized shall be entitled to take copies/extracts of seized records.

A **list of seized** goods or documents or records is required to be made by the officer and the person from whom the same are seized, shall be given a copy of the same.

Arrests

In the administration of taxation the provisions for arrests are created to tackle the situations created by unscrupulous tax evaders. Arrests are used in exceptional circumstance and only with prior authorization from the Commissioner.

A person can be arrested only if the tax amount is exceeding Rs. **100 lakhs**; and where the tax amount involved is more than Rs. **500 lakhs**, the offence is classified as cognizable and non-bailable and in such cases the bail can be considered by a Judicial Magistrate only.

<u>IMPORTANT DEFINITIONS (as defined in the Act)</u>

Person includes—

(*a*) an individual;

(*b*) a Hindu Undivided Family;

(*c*) a company;

(*d*) a firm;

(*e*) a Limited Liability Partnership;

(*f*) an AOP or BOI, whether incorporated or not, in India or outside India;

(*g*) any corporation established by or under any Central Act, State Act or Provincial Act or a Government company as defined in clause (*45*) of section 2 of the Companies Act, 2013;

(*h*) any body corporate incorporated by or under the laws of a country outside India;

(*i*) a co-operative society registered under any law relating to co-operative societies;

(*j*) a local authority;

(*k*) Central Government or a State Government;

(*l*) society as defined under the Societies Registration Act, 1860;

(*m*) trust; and

(*n*) every artificial juridical person, not falling within any of the above.

Business includes—

(*a*) any trade, commerce, manufacture, profession, vocation, adventure, wager or any other similar activity, whether or not it is for a pecuniary benefit;

(*b*) any activity or transaction in connection with or incidental or ancillary to above;

(*c*) any activity or transaction in the nature of point (*a*), whether or not there is volume, frequency, continuity or regularity of such transaction;

(*d*) supply or acquisition of goods including capital goods and services in connection with commencement or closure of business;

(*e*) provision by a club, association, society, or any such body (for a subscription or any other consideration) of the facilities or benefits to its members;

(*f*) admission, for a consideration, of persons to any premises;

(*g*) services supplied by a person as the holder of an office which has been accepted by him in the course or furtherance of his trade, profession or vocation;

(*h*) services provided by a race club by way of totalisator or licence to book maker in such club;

(*i*) any activity or transaction undertaken by the Central Government, a State Government or any local authority in which they are engaged as public authorities.

Business vertical means a distinguishable component of an enterprise that is engaged in the supply of individual goods or services or a group of related goods or services which is subject to *risks* and *returns* that are different from those of the other business verticals. This definition has been deleted now.

Consideration in relation to the supply of goods or services or both includes—

(*a*) any payment made or to be made, whether in money or otherwise, in respect of, in response to, or for the inducement of, the supply of goods or services or both, whether by the recipient or by any other person but shall not include any subsidy given by the Central Government or a State Government;

(*b*) the monetary value of any act or forbearance, in respect of, in response to, or for the inducement of, the supply of goods or services or both, whether by the recipient or by any other person but shall not include any subsidy given by the Central Government or a State Government.

Provided that a deposit given in respect of the supply of goods or services or both shall not be considered as payment made for such supply unless the supplier applies such deposit as consideration for the said supply.

Principal supply means the supply of goods or services which constitutes the predominant element of a composite supply and to which any other supply forming part of that composite supply is ancillary.

Exempt supply means supply of any goods or services or both which attracts NIL rate of tax or which may be wholly exempt from tax and includes non-taxable supply.

Non-taxable supply means a supply of goods or services or both which is not leviable to tax under GST act.

Family means —

(*i*) the spouse and children of the person, and

(*ii*) the parents, grand-parents, brothers and sisters of the person if they are wholly or mainly dependent on the said person.

Goods means every kind of movable property other than money and securities but includes actionable claim, growing crops, grass and things attached to or forming part of the land which are agreed to be severed before supply or under a contract of supply.

Movability and Marketability are the fundamental characteristic of goods.

Services means anything other than goods, money and securities but includes activities relating to the use of money or its conversion by cash or by any other mode, from one form, currency or denomination, to another form, currency or denomination for which a separate consideration is charged.

Capital goods means goods, the value of which is capitalised in the books of account of the person claiming the input tax credit and which are used or intended to be used in the course or furtherance of business.

Input means any goods other than capital goods used or intended to be used by a supplier in the course or furtherance of business.

Input service means any service used or intended to be used by a supplier in the course or furtherance of business.

Recipient of supply of goods or services or both, means—
(*a*) where a consideration is payable for the supply of goods or services or both, the person who is liable to pay that consideration;

(*b*) where no consideration is payable for the supply of goods, the person to whom the goods are delivered or made available, or to whom possession or use of the goods is given or made available; and

(*c*) where no consideration is payable for the supply of a service, the person to whom the service is rendered,

and any reference to a person to whom a supply is made shall be construed as a reference to the recipient of the supply and shall include an agent acting as such on behalf of the recipient in relation to the goods or services or both supplied.

Supplier in relation to any goods or services or both, shall mean the person supplying the said goods or services or both and shall include an agent acting as such on behalf of such supplier in relation to the goods or services or both supplied.

Manufacture means processing of raw material or inputs in any manner that results in emergence of a *new product* having a *distinct* name, character and use.

Removal in relation to goods, means—

(*a*) dispatch of the goods for delivery by the supplier thereof or by any other person acting on behalf of such supplier; or (*b*) collection of the goods by the recipient thereof or by any other person acting on behalf of such recipient.

Location of the recipient of services means,—

(*a*) where a supply is received at a place of business for which the **registration** has been obtained, the location of such place of business;

(*b*) where a supply is received at a place other than the place of business for which registration has been obtained (a fixed establishment elsewhere), the location of such fixed establishment;

(*c*) where a supply is received at more than one establishment, whether the place of business or fixed establishment, the location of the establishment most directly concerned with the receipt of the supply; and

(*d*) in absence of such places, the location of the usual place of residence of the recipient.

Location of the supplier of services means,—

(*a*) where a supply is made from a place of business for which the registration has been obtained, the location of such place of business;

(*b*) where a supply is made from a place other than the place of business for which registration has been obtained (a fixed establishment elsewhere), the location of such fixed establishment;
(*c*) where a supply is made from more than one establishment, whether the place of business or fixed establishment, the location of the establishment most directly concerned with the provisions of the supply; and

(*d*) in absence of such places, the location of the usual place of residence of the supplier.

Non-resident taxable person means any person who occasionally undertakes transactions involving supply of goods or services or both, whether as principal or agent or in any other capacity, but who has no fixed place of business or residence in India.

Fixed establishment means a place (other than the registered place of business) which is characterised by a sufficient degree of permanence and suitable structure in terms of human and technical resources to supply services, or to receive and use services for its own needs.

Place of business includes—

(*a*) a place from where the business is ordinarily carried on, and includes a warehouse, a godown or any other place where a taxable person stores his goods, supplies or receives goods or services or both; or

(*b*) a place where a taxable person maintains his books of account; or

(*c*) a place where a taxable person is engaged in business through an agent.

Usual place of residence means—

(*a*) in case of an individual, the place where he ordinarily resides;

(*b*) in other cases, the place where the person is incorporated or otherwise legally constituted.

Export of goods with its grammatical variations and cognate expressions, means taking goods out of India to a place outside India.

Import of goods with its grammatical variations and cognate expressions, means bringing goods into India from a place outside India.

Export of services means the supply of any service when,—

(i) the supplier of service is located in India;
(ii) the recipient of service is located outside India;
(iii) the place of supply of service is outside India;

(iv) the payment for such service has been received by the supplier of service in convertible foreign exchange; and
(v) the supplier of service and the recipient of service are not merely establishments of a distinct person.

Import of services means the supply of any service, where—

(i) the supplier of service is located outside India;
(ii) the recipient of service is located in India; and
(iii) the place of supply of service is in India;

Intermediary means a broker, an agent or any other person, by whatever name called, who arranges or facilitates the supply of goods or services or both, or securities, between two or more persons, but does not include a person who supplies such goods or services or both or securities on his own account.

Zero rated supply means any of the following supplies of goods or services or both, namely:—

(a) export of goods or services or both; or
(b) supply of goods or services or both to a Special Economic Zone developer or a Special Economic Zone unit.

Non-taxable online recipient means any Government, local authority, governmental authority, an individual or any other person not registered and receiving online information and database access or retrieval services in relation to any purpose other than commerce, industry or any other business or profession, located in taxable territory.

Online Information and Database Access or Retrieval Services means services whose delivery is mediated by information technology over the internet or an electronic network and the nature of which renders their supply essentially automated and involving minimal human intervention and impossible to ensure in the absence of information technology and includes electronic services such as:

(*i*) advertising on the internet;
(*ii*) providing cloud services;
(*iii*) provision of e-books, movie, music, software and other intangibles through telecommunication networks or internet;
(*iv*) providing data or information, retrievable or otherwise, to any person in electronic form through a computer network;
(*v*) online supplies of digital content (movies, television shows, music and the like);
(*vi*) digital data storage; and
(*vii*) online gaming.

Works Contract means a contract for building, construction, fabrication, completion, erection, installation, fitting out, improvement, modification, repair, maintenance, renovation, alteration or commissioning of any immovable property wherein transfer of property in goods (whether as goods or in some other form) is involved in the execution of such contract.

Government Entity shall mean an authority or a board or any other body including a society, trust, corporation, which is:

(a) set up by an Act of Parliament or State Legislature; or

(b) established by any Government,

with 90 percent or more participation by way of equity or control, to carry out a function entrusted by the Central Government, State government, Union territory or a local authority.